Feuding and Fighting

by
Martin Herbert

BPS BOOKS   THE BRITISH PSYCHOLOGICAL SOCIETY

First published in 1996 by BPS Books (The British Psychological Society), St Andrews House, 48 Princess Road East, Leicester LE1 7DR, UK.

© Martin Herbert, 1996

A catalogue record for this book is available from the British Library.

ISBN 1 85433 191 4

Whilst every effort has been made to ensure the accuracy of the contents of this publication, the publishers and author expressly disclaim responsibility in law for negligence or any other cause of action whatsoever.

Typeset by Ralph Footring, Derby.

Printed in Great Britain by Stanley L. Hunt Printers Ltd., Rushden, Northants.

Contents

Feuding and fighting

Introduction

Parents use the phrase 's/he is a terrible problem' most often when talking about their child's disobedience and aggression. It is the latter trait, one of the main disciplinary headaches that beset children's caregivers, that is the particular concern of this guide.

Aims

The aims of this guide are:

➤ to provide practitioners with information about childhood aggression and its development;

➤ to help practitioners work out some strategic plans with the child's parents about their own attitudes to aggression and other disciplinary problems;

➤ to provide workable, practical methods – *disciplinary tactics* – which parents can use to manage quarrels and other forms of aggressive behaviour displayed by their children.

Objectives

In order to teach parents these skills, after reading this guide you should be able to:

➤ differentiate, by means of developmental information, normal assertiveness and aggression from extreme variations of behaviour which hold potentially more worrying, long-term implications;

➤ identify predisposing influences on the development of coercive, aggressive problems;

➤ carry out a functional (ABC) analysis, based on social learning theory, of the antecedents and consequences of current aggressive behaviours; that is, the circumstances that trigger and maintain such activities;

➤ plan, initiate and follow up a programme (in collaboration with the parents) to pre-empt or reduce problematic (that is, dysfunctional) aggression.

The raised consciousness brought about by intense public and professional concern regarding child and spouse abuse has had the effect of many people assuming that violence to women and children is the most common and most problematic aspect of violence in the home. Yet much more common is violence between siblings – so commonplace that the public rarely perceives it as family violence. This is somewhat surprising, given the mounting tide of public concern about bullying and other forms of violence carried out by children and adolescents, on the streets and in the schools.

Aggressive children make their parents suffer and they make their teachers suffer. Other children, particularly the less robust ones, also suffer at their hands, their feet and the rough edges of their tongues. In turn, parents of the 'victims' have to cope with their offspring's tears and anxieties about going to school, out to play or to places where they will meet with bullying or abuse. Aggressive children, who are in many cases frustrated and abused children themselves, eventually hurt themselves too; the unhappiness which makes them aggressive is compounded when they are shunned by other youngsters and punished by adults.

The trouble with terms such as 'aggression' is that they contain so many meanings and cover so many different activities. Studies of aggression in individuals and societies indicate that there is no *instinctive* impulse towards violence in human beings. The feeling of anger may well be aroused by involuntary processes, but humans are not programmed in their behavioural responses to the emotion. Aggressiveness is a *learned* habit or appetite, hence the fascinating variety of possibilities in human behaviours.

Social rather than biological characteristics influence, in the main, the hostile acts and belligerence of individuals. This has infused the debates of successive generations about the malignant effects of penny dreadfuls, comics, the movies, television and, of late, video nasties, with much solemnity, sometimes even amounting to moral panic.

The development of aggressive behaviour

Much of a child's aggressiveness arises as a natural, if tiresome, side-effect of becoming socialized (the process of acquiring knowledge, values and skills to allow integration into society). From birth onwards there are individual differences in assertiveness and passivity which tend to persist as children grow older. For example, rage appears in very young infants, when the infant hits out because of frustration at the thwarting of his/her desires. Typical displays of undirected anger in young children include jumping up and down, breath-holding and screaming. The younger the child, the stronger their demands for the immediate gratification of their wants. As the child gets older, random, undirected or unfocused displays of emotional excitement become rarer, and aggression that is retaliatory becomes more frequent. This may manifest itself in throwing objects, grabbing, pinching, biting, striking, calling names, arguing and insisting.

It is not easy for young children to learn to 'wait patiently', 'ask nicely', or to be generous, considerate and self-sacrificing. From early on children have a repertoire of some 14 *coercive* behaviours, including temper tantrums, crying, whining, yelling and commanding, which they use (wittingly or unwittingly) to influence their parents. At times this influence develops into outright manipulation and confrontation. Coercive behaviours decline steadily in frequency from a high point around the age of two (the 'terrible twos') to more moderate levels by the age of school entrance.

The older aggressive boy or girl displays coercive behaviours at a level similar to those of a two- or three-year-old child and, in this sense, is an exemplar of arrested socialization. What usually happens is that with increasing age, certain coercive behaviours, such as whining, crying and tantrums, are no longer acceptable to parents; these behaviours then become the target for monitoring and sanctions, which are in turn accompanied by reductions in their frequency and intensity.

By the age of four, there are substantial improvements in a child's ability to hold in check their negative commands, destructiveness and attempts to coerce by aggressive means. By five, most children use less negativism, non-compliance, and negative physical actions than their younger siblings, and such an increase in self-control in the maturing child is most welcome to parents. Nevertheless, at the age of nine, more than 50 per cent of boys, but only 30 per cent of girls, are still having quite frequent explosions of temper. Some of the differences in aggressiveness between boys and girls may be due to the fact that parents in western cultures tend to disapprove more of aggression in girls than in boys.

When is aggressiveness a problem?

Given the fact that all children display aggressive behaviour as they mature, at what point can aggression (or, indeed, any other misbehaviour) be judged to be excessive, counterproductive and thus dysfunctional? Our mental alarm bells should begin to ring if the frequency and/or intensity, or persistence (duration) of the aggressive behaviour seem to be extreme. Our concern would increase also if there were many other coexisting problems such as defiance, destructiveness and hyperactivity. Figure 1 illustrates this.

	Frequency –	high rates of aggressive behaviour
	Intensity –	extreme, for example, cruel or bullying actions, or persistent (intractable) violence
Behaviour	Number –	several coexisting problems
	Duration –	long enduring 'chronic' difficulties
	Sense/meaning –	bizarre, un-understandable, for example, sadistic, behaviour.

Figure 1: FINDS diagram

Loss of parental control

Many parents feel bruised and abused (literally and figuratively, physically and emotionally) by their children and teenagers. Others remain silent, too embarrassed to admit the harassment and, not infrequently, fear, they experience daily. I have worked with adolescents whose hatred for their parents spilled over regularly into verbal abuse (obscenities, humiliating criticism and threats) and physical assaults (ranging from slaps to serious violence). Researchers into family violence make the point that the very notion of children controlling, indeed, *assaulting*, their parents is so alien to our ideas about the relationships between parents and their offspring that it is difficult to believe that such a reversal, especially one so subversive, can actually occur.

Clinical observations of children and adolescents who exert continuing and extreme defiance of, or intimidation (including physical assaults) towards, parents, indicate that most of these families have some disturbance in the authority structure within the family. The children in these families may develop a grandiose sense of self, feel omnipotent, and expect everyone to respond to them accordingly (Herbert, 1987a). Not surprisingly, their siblings are also likely to come within their line of fire.

Prevention of aggressive behaviour

Children with problems of this order, seem to be arrested at a demanding (*egocentric*) stage of development, whatever their physical age may be. The period between approximately one and three years of age is a sensitive period with regard to the development (and therefore prevention) of such conduct. These problems take root because of the inability of parents, for a variety of reasons, to confront their child's early and 'natural' coercive behaviour in a manner that will launch him/her into the vital later stages of social development and those aspects of socialization which have to do with co-operation, empathy and impulse control.

The psychologist Gerald Patterson (1982) suggests (*inter alia*) the following reasons for a child's failure to substitute more mature behaviours for his/her primitive coercive repertoire:

➢ the parents may neglect to teach *prosocial skills* (for example, by seldom reinforcing (by praising or in other words encouraging) the child's use of language or other self-help skills);

➢ the parents may, however, reinforce the child's display of coercive behaviours by attending to it, giving in to it, or in other ways providing it with a 'payoff';

➢ brothers and sisters may be allowed to tease or bully the child in such a manner that the only way s/he can stop them is by answering like with like, namely, through coercive behaviours;

➢ the parents may use punishment inconsistently when dealing with coercive behaviours;

➢ when parents *do* punish, they are likely to do so in a feeble manner that lacks credibility.

What is it like to live in a family environment which lacks boundaries, which does not set limits? Children are not capable of providing those boundaries for themselves in any rational manner. The outcome is insecurity and a series of explosive responses to situations for which no clearly understood family rules exist (Bolton and Bolton, 1987).

As children approach adolescence and grow stronger, more assertive and more rebellious, what were merely *difficult* situations for parents can become menacing, and in some cases, dangerous, especially where the children have been granted too much control over decisions.

To address the question of *why* self-defeating or other offending behaviours such as aggression are initiated and maintained (the issue of *causation*), behaviourally orientated professionals conduct a comprehensive functional analysis of the child's (or caregiver's) behaviour relating it to events and contingencies in two environments, external and internal (*organismic*) (Herbert, 1987b). Before attempting to answer the 'why?' question it is essential to be clear and precise about *what* one is attempting to explain.

Part I: Assessment

The first stage involves a painstaking investigation of the parameters (the *why?*, *where?*, *when?* and *how?*) of the problem(s), once specified. There are psychological screening/assessment instruments to help us in this task (see Herbert, 1987b; 1993; Webster-Stratton and Herbert, 1994). *Appendix I* provides a recording form to help with this task.

The second stage, the 'why?' question, falls into two parts:

(1) predisposing (historical) influences; and
(2) precipitating (instigating, triggering) and reinforcing events.

In the terms of social learning theory, aggressive antisocial behaviour and interactions are regarded as a function of the combination of somatic factors, previous learning experiences, and contemporary events. The assessment of these events is a matter of identifying precisely the *antecedent*, *consequences*, and *symbolic conditions* (for example, beliefs, attitudes) which control the problem behaviour. There are several possibilities:

➤ problem behaviour may be a response to certain precursors — antecedent conditions which elicit or reinforce that behaviour;
➤ there may be certain outcome conditions which either reinforce or punish *problem behaviour* or prosocial behaviour;
➤ any of these inappropriate forms of antecedent or outcome control may be operating in the child's thinking (symbolic) processes rather than in his/her external environment or physiological changes. For example, there may be an impairment of his/her problem-solving capacity.

The above-mentioned analysis is sometimes referred to as the **ABC of behaviour**; it represents a relatively simple way of 'teasing out' the manner in which children *learn* to behave badly.

The ABC of behaviour

This is where the ABC of behaviour will prove useful (an example is given in *Appendix II*).

A   stands for *Antecedents* or what set the stage for (what led up to) the
B   which stands for *Behaviour* (or what the child actually does), while
C   refers to the *Consequences* (or what occurred immediately after the behaviour).

Meaningful stimuli (the A term) are vital because they direct our behaviour. Or to put this another way, it is crucial for the individual's survival that s/he *learns* to respond appropriately to stimuli. For instance, we can rely on most car drivers to respond to the stimulus of a red traffic light by stopping. If we could not, chaos would ensue. We can depend on the vast majority of parents to respond to the stimulus of a crying child by caring for her/his needs; otherwise children would not survive.

Psychological 'laws' often take the form of statements about the relationship between events called stimuli, and responses. These are called stimulus–response (S–R) laws: 'Given stimulus A, one would expect response B'. Or more economically: 'If A, then B'. We can make use of these laws to make reasonable predictions about adult and child behaviour in given situations and conditions, and are thus in a position to suggest ways of changing behaviour that has gone wrong, as in the case of extreme aggressiveness. Many of the connections or associations between stimuli and responses are learned on the basis of imitation (modelling) or conditioning processes.

Antecedents

There are different types of antecedent influence on learning. Of particular importance, in childhood, is the form of learning based on imitation or modelling.

Experiments and observations have convincingly illustrated how children imitate not only desirable behaviour, but also inappropriate actions. In one study, those nursery-children who had observed aggressive models displayed a great number of precisely imitated aggressive responses, which rarely occurred in the other ('control') group who had observed non-aggressive models. In addition, the results indicated that models observed on film were as effective as real-life models in transmitting hostile patterns of behaviour.

This example is a very simple one, but even such apparently simple patterns of learning are difficult to analyse. Psychologists are not certain why some models (but not others) have an almost irresistible influence over children.

Consequences

If the consequence (the C term) of a behaviour is rewarding (that is, favourable) to a child, that behaviour is likely to increase in strength. For example, it may become more frequent! Put another way: if James does something, such as sharing his toys rather than quarrelling over them, and as a result of his action something pleasant happens to him, then he is more likely to do the same thing in similar circumstances in the future. When psychologists refer to this pleasant outcome as the 'positive reinforcement' of behaviour, they have in mind several kinds of reinforcers: *tangible* rewards (for example, sweets, treats, pocket money); *social* rewards (for example, attention, a smile, a pat on the back, a word of encouragement); and *self-reinforcers* (the ones that come from within and which are non-tangible, such as self-praise, self-approval, a sense of pleasure). For instance, if you say 'James, that was nice of you to let your sister have a turn on your bike, I am very pleased with you', James is more likely to lend his bicycle again. (Note: we are dealing in *probabilities* not certainties).

Here then, is a form of learning (*instrumental* or *operant conditioning/learning*) in which the frequency of a behaviour (which occurs quite spontaneously in the individual) is increased by following its appearance with a reward (that is, by reinforcing it). If it does not occur spontaneously, you will have to *prompt* it, and then *reinforce* it.

If the interval is too long, learning does not occur. It is of little use promising a young child a reward which won't eventuate for a week; it is not likely to have much incentive or teaching value. Long deferred punishments, likewise, are ineffectual. Of course, older children are better able to understand delayed incentives. Symbolic rewards such as stars or other stickers on a chart, bridge the gap between action and a promised reward, such as a special outing.

In day-to-day situations, it is only on the odd occasion that the mother says 'good boy' or smiles in approval when her child behaves appropriately or well. In fact, there is evidence that what is referred to as 'intermittent reinforcement' (the occasional reward) is a more potent method for *maintaining* the frequency of desirable behaviour than reinforcement presented for every 'correct' response made. The manufacturers of 'one armed bandits' (fruit machines) have cleverly used this principle in the schedules of reinforcement programmed into the machines. You win just often enough to keep you at that machine.

Negative reinforcement also facilitates/increases behaviour by removing an unpleasant consequence ('If you don't stop teasing your sister you won't be allowed to watch your television programme').

Family influences

The way in which parents manage their child's aggressive behaviour (in terms of modelling, reinforcement history, and so on) can have an important bearing, in the long run, on whether s/he is too submissive or too hostile. Some children are on a short fuse, quick to anger; every small provocation is welcomed as an opportunity to release a flood of hostile acts or verbal abuse. Others are slow to react and find it easy to sit out frustrating events.

Family factors have been implicated in the manifestation of bullying behaviour, most clearly in Norwegian research (see Olweus, 1989). Sibling abuse (and the aggression, which if intense and persistent can be thought of as abuse) is quite likely to occur in the home that already knows child abuse at the hands of the parent. Exposure to an aggressive parent, combined with a general background lacking warmth or positive affect, can result in children experiencing difficulty in controlling their own aggressive impulses. In the case of children who bully others, whether inside or outside the home, there seems to be an association with cold, as opposed to warm, child-rearing, intense levels of discord or violence in the home, and a lack of clear rules about discipline, or the monitoring of aggressive or other behaviour (Herbert, 1987a; Patterson, 1982). Children growing up in such families have bullying behaviours to imitate, with little counteracting identification with caregivers who provide affection and/or training in self-restraint.

Several studies have demonstrated the difficulties that aggressive children experience in decoding social messages given to them by family and peers and their tendency to minimize perceptions of their own aggressiveness, while maximizing those of others (notably their peers). A number of cross-sectional and longitudinal studies (see Webster-Stratton and Herbert, 1994, for a review) have focused on the importance of individual sociodemographic variables such as family size, number of siblings, socioeconomic status, parental absence, parental criminality or other abnormal individual characteristics. There seems to be a consensus in a variety of studies that aggressive behaviour in children can be related to broad (long-term) attitudes and child-rearing practices.

As we have seen, a combination of lax discipline (especially with regard to the offspring's acts of aggression), combined with hostile attitudes in the parents, produces very aggressive and poorly controlled behaviour in the offspring (Herbert, 1987a). Parents with hostile attitudes are generally unaccepting and disapproving of children: they fail to give affection, understanding or explanations to children, and tend to use a lot of physical punishment without giving reasons. When they do exert their authority, it is usually applied erratically and arbitrarily. Such methods are often referred to as *power-assertive*: the adult asserts dominant and authoritarian control through physical punishment, harsh verbal abuse, angry threats and deprivation of privileges. There is a positive relationship between the extensive use of physical punishment in the home by parents and high levels of aggression in their offspring outside the home. Violence begets violence; what the child appears to learn is that might is right.

Ineffectual discipline and communication

The communication, cues and unspoken messages in the homes of aggressive/conduct-disordered children are frequently negative ones, incessant criticism, nagging, crying and shouting. Patterson (*op. cit.*) refers to much of it as 'ineffectual nattering' on the part of the parents. His position, and he qualifies it carefully, is that the control of antisocial behaviour requires the timely use of some kind of punishment. But why doesn't aggressive behaviour diminish or disappear, as would be predicted from learning theory?

The answer is that it is not *punishment per se,* but the *kind* of punishment used by the parents of aggressive children that may be ineffective. There is a case to be made for the necessity of punishing aggressive child behaviours, but in the context of a warm, loving relationship where reasoning and explanations are used in conjunction with *nonviolent punishment*. (Parents need to be reminded that reasoning with a child in an agitated, angry state is not only ineffective, it is actually counterproductive.) Patterson holds this view of punishment based upon his conclusions arising from two decades of evaluated intervention with families of aggressive children.

Disciplinary methods, such as time-out and logical consequences (for example, extra work in the home or loss of privileges), are definitely aversive; however, they are *not* violent (see pages 29 and 39, respectively), and Patterson vouches for their relative effectiveness. Certainly there is overwhelming evidence that extremes of physical punishment, particularly when perpetrated against a background of uncaring indifference or outright rejection, constitute the slippery slope for the creation of a violent youngster (Herbert, 1987a).

Poor limit-setting by parents

Among the critical antecedents to examine in the assessment of noncompliant, aggressive behaviour are the *rules* (implicit and explicit) enforced at home and school. These include the conventional rules of good manners and correct behaviour toward particular persons or situations, rules that involve sympathy and respect for others, keeping faith, helping, and honesty (Herbert, 1987a; 1989). Some of these are about good manners; others are moral rules which are essential (many people would insist) to the maintenance of social order and a civilized life. The induction of the child into the social system (socialization) involves the transmission to the child of social *and* moral codes by the family and other agents of society.

An important issue in assessment, given the defiance of rules by conduct-disordered children, is thus the nature of the boundaries and limits established by parents for their children. In this sense, boundaries are defined by 'rules' which specify an individual's role within the family, the subsystem s/he belongs to, and the appropriate behaviours which such membership entails. Boundaries can be clear (because the rules are easily recognized and accepted), diffuse (ambiguous and chaotic because rules are unstable or absent), or rigid (where rules are inflexible, unadaptable).

Behavioural family therapists are especially concerned to assess those areas where families manifest weak boundaries or reversed roles between generations, a condition in which conduct problems flourish (Herbert, 1987a; 1993). For example, parents may be 'obedient' to un-reasonable demands from their offspring; in such cases the child usurps the role of the parent by taking control in the home to such an extent that the boundaries between parent and child roles are not clear.

The consequences of ingrained patterns of child care such as these tend to be lasting. In West and Farrington's study of London boys (to take one example), substantial continuity was evident (West and Farrington, 1973). Of the youths rated most aggressive at 8 to 10 years old, 50 per cent were still in the most aggressive group at 12 to 14 years old (compared with 19 per cent of the remaining boys in the study) and 40 per cent were so at 16 to 18 years (compared with 27 per cent of the remainder). The boys who were severely aggressive at 8 to 10 years were especially likely to become violent delinquents (14 per cent vs. 4.5 per cent).

Patterson and his collaborators at the Oregon Social Learning Center (*op. cit.*), observing in great detail the behaviour of aggressive children at home, found that their families differed from the families of normal children in a number of ways:

➤ the parents of aggressive children showed a lack of consistency in disciplining their children;

➤ although the parents used punishment very often, this was inefficient either because it was not clearly associated with transgression or because, when the child counterattacked, the parents finally gave in to his/her demands;

➤ lack of supervision or monitoring; aggressive children were more frequently left on their own;

➤ parents of aggressive children were described as lacking warmth, unable to involve themselves in pleasant shared activities or to clearly show their children what is right and what is wrong or what they were expected to do or not to do in any situation;

➤ mothers of aggressive children were likely to identify *themselves* as victims of their child's hostile aggression.

By way of contrast with the adverse life influences just described, the factors that *facilitate* the development of social awareness and adaptive behaviour include:

➤ strong ties of affection between parents and children;

➤ firm moral demands made by parents on their offspring;

➤ the consistent use of sanctions (setting limits);

➤ techniques of punishment that are psychological rather than physical (that is, methods that signify or threaten withdrawal of approval), thus provoking anxiety or guilt rather than anger;

➤ an intensive use of reasoning and explanations (inductive methods);

➤ giving responsibility.

The balancing of these attributes is perhaps best illustrated in the philosophy of what, on the basis of her investigations, Baumrind (1971) calls the 'authoritative' parent. S/he is clear about the limits or behavioural boundaries set for the child, but they are not narrow or unreasonable. S/he gives the child choices and explanations, but is adamant, firm (not authoritarian) in requiring the child's compliance to social and moral rules, some of which are negotiable.

However, if a child is subjected to frequent critical evaluations by family members it leads to poor self-image, resulting in a predisposition to act aggressively, particularly in threatening interpersonal situations. In this situation children use aggressive behaviour to terminate aversive (unpleasant) interactions by their parents or other members of the family. This process is neatly described by Patterson (*op. cit.*) in terms of what he refers to as the 'coercive family process'.

The coercive family process

This theory postulates that aggressive, conduct-disordered children engage in excessive rates of behaviour which are aversive for parents who, in turn, retaliate with equally excessive rates of aversive actions which lead on to an upwardly escalating spiral of unremitting sound and fury – tantrums, shouting, screaming and, perhaps, hitting. Such interactions are negatively reinforcing both to the aggressive children and to the parents; children are reinforced by their parents' eventual compliance. It is difficult in these circumstances to know what is cause and what is effect. In terms of the development of antisocial behaviour these processes can be conceptualized as a series of positive feedback loops; inept parenting fosters antisocial child behaviour and deficits in the child's skills; these are characteristics which, in turn, make child-rearing more difficult for the parents, and so on.

Negative reinforcement

Parents (with the help of practitioners) would be well advised to look out for the accidental strengthening of undesirable behaviours by *negative reinforcement* of them. This means that any actions that will 'turn off' an unpleasant (aversive) event are strengthened. Most of us learn to avoid or escape from painful events. Here is a fairly typical sequence:

Tom annoys Chris by grabbing his toy — Chris reacts by hitting Tom — Tom then stops annoying Chris, thus negatively reinforcing Chris's hitting response.

Chris has coerced Tom into terminating his annoying behaviour. A vicious coercive spiral is quite likely to be set in motion, an escalation of attack and counter-attack. To continue the sequence:

➢   Tom may react to Chris's hitting not by desisting from grabbing at Chris's toy, but by hitting back in an attempt to terminate Chris's aggression — Chris now responds to Tom's aggression with more intense counter-aggression.

This exchange would continue until it was interrupted by an irritated parent or until one of the antagonists was negatively reinforced by the cessation of warfare on the part of the other child. We can see how it carries within it the seeds for a beginning and perpetuation of bullying behaviour in the child's repertoire.

One of the ironies you will find, if you try to analyse the ABC sequences (see following) of some of your clients' confrontations with their children, is that they may be strengthening behaviours that they do not like and weakening (extinguishing) actions that they would really wish to encourage. Here is an example: Pauline is arguing with her older brother – she wants the paintbox he is using. She whines and demands the paints. John refuses, so Pauline puts a few more decibels into a louder, higher-pitched whine. Irritated beyond words, Mother orders John to hand over the paints to his 'poor little sister'. She has reinforced Pauline for whining and made the future use of such coercive behaviour more likely. Getting the paintbox is the reinforcer.

But that is not all, unfortunately. Mother has also been reinforced by 'turning off' that distressing whiny noise. The relief (a reward) has made likely the future likelihood of 'giving in' to whining. Doubtless she would be quite indignant if we told her she was 'training' her child to be whiny, and that Pauline was training *her* to take the unjust line of least resistance.

These are the kinds of causal sequences (among other sources of information) it is useful to elicit from parents/carers. The assessment process (a functional analysis) for one relatively simple form of aggression temper tantrums is illustrated in the following.

The ABC (functional) analysis

Step 1: Identify the parent's perception of the problem

For example:

Parent: Aisha has a temper tantrum when I insist that she obeys me; for example, when I tell her to eat breakfast. This happens every morning. With me, not her father.

Step 2: Identify the child's assets

For example:

Therapist: You have pointed out some of your problems with Aisha. If we look at this form you will see that it has a credit and debit column. I've listed on the debit side all of her behaviours that you find unacceptable; now let us list her good points on the credit side.

Step 3: Identify desired outcomes (goals)

For example:

Therapist: If you were to wake up one morning to find that Aisha has changed for the better, how would you know? What would be different about her behaviour or attitude? Would you want anything in the family to be different so as to make life easier or more contented? (Other members of the family should also be given an opportunity to comment in a similar manner).

Step 4: Work out and observe the ABC of behaviour/beliefs/interactions

For example:

Therapist: Before you can change your child's behaviour you have to look at that behaviour very closely; also your own and that of other members of the family. What sets the stage for the undesirable behaviours you wish to change? These, you have said, are frequent bouts of aggression. What, at the time, are your feelings – you mentioned helplessness? How do you react? What consequences flow from these confrontations? (See *Appendix II*).

At this stage the ABC model is explained, verbally and/or with a handout (see p. 37). For example:

Therapist: When experience leads to a relatively permanent change of behaviour, attitude, or knowledge, we say that learning has occurred. Memorizing a formula, recognizing a face, reading music, being scared of doing maths or going to parties, are all examples of learning. We have to distinguish between *learning* an action or behaviour and actually *performing* it. A child may learn something but not do it. Reward is anything that makes a child's actions worthwhile! A behaviour will be more likely to happen again if it has favourable consequences; it will be less likely to occur again if it is not followed by a reward – what, technically, we call 'positive reinforcement'. Also if it is penalized. If your child does something you do not like, such as losing his/her temper too easily, you may increase his/her ability to think first and hold their temper by either *rewarding* them (with words of praise) for maintaining self-control and/or by consistently applying the sanctions (penalties) you consistently apply for his/her failing to do so.

Step 5: Specify the target behaviours

For example:

Therapist: Remember the ABC of behaviour which we have discussed. The B term stands for *behaviour* (Aisha's temper tantrums in this instance), and it also stands for *beliefs* (your feelings and attitudes about what is happening in this instance). Let us be clear about what you are going to observe at home and elsewhere. So what is it that Aisha *does* and *says* that makes you call her actions and words a 'temper tantrum'?

Parent: Aisha stamps her foot, clenches his fists, kicks the chairs. She also screams and swears.

Step 6: Observe the frequency of the target behaviours

For example:

Therapist: I want you to count the number of tantrums (defined by those actions you described) that Aisha has per day. (You could also time how long each episode lasts.) Do this for three or four days.

Step 7: Look at the ABC of behaviour

For example:

Therapist: I want you to keep a diary record of some of the episodes, with particular emphasis on the ABC sequence.

Here is an example of Aisha's mother's formulation of an ABC sequence.

A I was waiting my turn at the checkout counter at the supermarket. Aisha kept putting chocolates in the basket. I kept taking them out. She said, 'I want a sweet!' I said, 'No love, you can have a biscuit when we get home'. She said loudly, 'Give me a bloody sweet!' I asked her to please not make a fuss.

B She began to scream and kick the counter; then she lay down on the floor, blocking the counter so other people couldn't get to it.

C Everyone was looking at me and I felt so embarrassed I gave her a chocolate and said, 'Just wait till we get home…!' She quieted down immediately and began to eat it. I felt very angry, resentful, and humiliated.

Therapist: And then?
Parent: I said no more at home, to keep the peace.

Step 8: Analyse your information: antecedents

For example:
Therapist: When you look at your diary after a few days, and your tally of tantrums, are they part of a more general pattern? Are the As, the antecedents, rather similar?
Parent: Yes, they seem to form a pattern of defiance. They follow two lines. Either Aisha commands me to do something, and if I don't, she insists, and eventually has a tantrum. Or I ask Aisha to do something, she ignores me or says 'I won't', and if I insist, she has a tantrum.

Step 9: Be specific about the problem behaviour

For example:
Therapist: When you look at your tally, do the tantrums seem more frequent:

➢ at certain times?
➢ in certain places?
➢ with certain people?
➢ in particular situations?

Parent: The answer in this case is yes to all those questions. They are most frequent in the morning and at night; in the bedroom and at the dinner table; with me; when I try to dress her, get her to play with her brother, or share her toys with him. I can see that Aisha usually gets her own way ... not always, but nearly always. She also gets me going. I sometimes end up in tears. She always gets me into an argument and I have to devote a lot of time to the dispute.
Therapist: Who were you really observing? The answer inevitably will be not only your child. You are observing, as part of your analysis of As and Cs – in the ABC sequences – your child in relation to yourself **and** others. It is not possible to understand a child's behaviour without looking at the influence of other people on her, and her influence on them. In this instance, you (and others) have unwittingly reinforced (strengthened) the very behaviours (tantrums)

that you wished to reduce in frequency. For example, one reinforcer is that she gets her own way; the second is that she riles you and enjoys winding you up; the third reinforcer is that she monopolizes your attention; even if it is scolding, it is rewarding. You know that it is rewarding and not punishing because the behaviour is as persistent as ever.

To change Aisha's behaviour we will have to plan a small programme in which you reinforce her for appropriate behaviour which we'll define carefully (sharing would be one example), and ignore, where feasible, or penalize, temper tantrums and other inappropriate behaviours in ways which we'll discuss (see pages 35–41).

Part II: Assessing sibling quarrels

Sibling rivalry

Out of the blue, small children will horrify their parents by their outspoken jealousy, sometimes asking hopefully: 'When is *it* going away?' (the 'it' being the new baby). Sibling rivalry is the name psychologists give to the often rancorous competition between brothers and sisters. Some individuals continue this sibling rivalry into adult life, and their competition with colleagues and opponents has all the intensity and fierceness of half-forgotten rivalries from childhood. Almost every child has some feelings of envy and rejection when they have to compete with a new baby (or a more active toddler) who demands so much of mother's attention. S/he may feel unloved or 'cast off' in favour of the brother or sister, however unjustified these feelings may be. The jealousy is often accompanied by attention-seeking infantile behaviour as if s/he can only compete for the previous monopoly position by becoming a baby again.

Sibling rivalry is considered a 'normal' part of relations between brothers and sisters; indeed, many parents believe that such rivalry provides a good training ground for the successful management of aggressive behaviour in the real world. American parents generally feel that some exposure to aggression is a positive experience that should occur early in life; seven out of ten Americans agreed with the statement 'When a boy is growing up it is important for him to have a few fist fights'.

Prevalence

Susan Steinmetz (1987), in her study of sibling conflict in intact Delaware families, found that between 63 per cent and 68 per cent of adolescents in the families she studied used physical force to resolve conflicts with their brothers and sisters. Sociologists who have studied aggression between brothers and sisters report that parents feel it is important for their children to learn how to handle themselves in violent situations and do not actively discourage their children from becoming involved in disputes with their siblings. In fact, parents may try to ignore aggressive interactions and only become involved when minor situations are perceived as about to escalate into major confrontations.

There is a view, which is both popular and respectable (although unproven), that childhood fighting and games of murder and mayhem, and also the watching of portrayed violence, can exert a positive effect through catharsis. Emotions, according to this theory, are purged because of the release of tension involved in sibling quarrels or in identifying with the participants in a representation of violent events. Anger is drained off, so to speak, by 'living through' (in imagination) or 'acting out' these situations. Some parents argue that it is alright for children to express aggression towards their parents (or siblings) because they frustrate them; this channelling and direct expression of anger is supposed to be 'healthier' than its inhibition.

There are at least two reasons to question the assumptions underlying such notions – the pressure-cooker metaphor. The first is that there is little place in civilized, co-operative living for direct and primitive expressions of aggression, when aggression is thought of as either physical or verbal attack. Certain disguised verbal aggression, such as teasing, gossip, or 'frankness', are condoned to a greater degree than physical attack or direct verbal abuse, but even gossip and frankness that conceal hostility are more likely to produce complications in human relations than to ease or facilitate social interaction.

Second, learning theory predicts that the expression of aggression and its consequent momentary tension-relief strengthens, rather than weakens, the tendency to behave aggressively. There is evidence to support this prediction (see Herbert, 1991). Nor does evidence indicate that behaving aggressively *reduces* tendencies to be aggressive; if anything, available studies suggest that the opposite is true. Whatever the evidence, public opinion seems remarkably philosophical, indeed, complacent, about manifestations of aggression.

Steinmetz found that it was sometimes difficult to get parents to discuss sibling violence, not because they were ashamed or embarrassed to admit such behaviour, but because they simply did not view their children's actions much of the time as abusive or even worthy of mentioning. The parents in 49 families recorded the frequency and types of aggressive interaction between their offspring during a one-week period: a total of 131 sibling conflicts occurred during this period, ranging from short-lived arguments to more serious confrontations. This figure, although high, is probably a considerable underestimation of the *true* extent of sibling aggression.

Dunn and Kendrick (1982) observed directly the interactions of English children (brothers and sisters) in their own homes. In each of 43 pairs of siblings, the younger child was 18 months old. The mothers' actions were also recorded. They revisited six months later to make further observations and discovered that:

➤ there was a good deal of quarrelling – an average of about eight fights, or potential fights per hour;

➤ the mother's intrusion in quarrels led to more conflict over the longer term. In families where the mother tended to intervene, often in the first observation period, the children did have longer quarrels and more frequent physical fights in the second observation period (six months later) than in families where she intervened less;

➤ when a mother adopted a style of discussing rules and feelings with her children when they quarrelled, she was apt to develop in her offspring more mature ways of handling conflict. These included conciliatory actions, such as showing concern for, comforting, helping or apologizing to the other. Her children were more likely to refer to rules – 'We have to take turns. Mummy said so'.

It is sometimes argued that quarrelling might well increase in frequency if each child observed the other being reprimanded or getting the parent even temporarily to take his/her side. The counter-argument is that parental intervention is necessary to teach values of fair play, sharing and compromise. Many parents feel, too, that if they *don't* intervene, injury and/or an injustice could be inflicted on the younger and/or weaker child. Nor do they wish to condone the use of fighting or bullying by default, which means inaction.

Parental intervention in sibling quarrels

Dunn (see Dunn and Kendrick, 1982) has reviewed several studies of parental intervention and non-intervention. Studies in which parents were trained to stay right out of brotherly and sisterly quarrels seem to indicate that the frequency of such arguments can be reduced, particularly if ignoring quarrels is combined with rewarding the children for desisting from conflict. Other studies indicate that if parents wish to encourage in their children an ability to care about what happens to other people, they need to point out clearly and forcefully to their offspring, when young, the consequences of being unkind and aggressive. Dunn comments that quarrels between brothers and sisters provide the ideal training-ground to carry out this kind of teaching, although it can be an uphill struggle. Interviews with young children indicate that they use far more emotional words to describe their brothers and sisters than to describe friends or even parents. More often than not the words they choose to apply are negative.

A large variety of unpleasant events (*aversive stimuli*) can set the stage for the development of conflict and a chain reaction of quarrelsome behaviours – for example, bullying and teasing of a painful, threatening or humiliating nature; or depriving the weaker child of his/her property, rights and opportunities. Dunn found that two-year-old, second-born children were just as likely as their elders to initiate a quarrel, to tease, and to hit. Mothers were twice as likely to scold the older children and tell them to stop; with younger children, however, they tended not to scold but to distract them and try to interest them in something other than the source of conflict.

Rivalry between children

Rivalry between children can be useful in spurring them on to greater efforts, so long as the competition does not become too intense. It is important for parents not to compare children's achievements directly, but to show that each is an individual with his/her own special talents – one may be good at sport, be good at fixing things, may sing well and also have a way with animals. If parents set their levels of aspiration too high – beyond the child's capacity – it will affect the child's self-esteem adversely. If s/he suffers from low self-esteem, s/he will be vulnerable to failure and then may withdraw, if possible, from the challenging activity. To some youngsters, failure acts as an incentive to try harder; to others, it merely confirms an existing conclusion that they are 'no good'. Their fear of failure becomes so pervasive that they throw in the sponge before meeting the challenge.

The bright sibling expects to succeed, hence success and praise do not surprise him/her nor do they raise him/her to new levels of performance. S/he does not expect to fail or be criticized; hence when such things happen, the effect is salutary. The sanction, as it were, is so telling that s/he redoubles his/her efforts to avoid encountering it again. This is *not* to suggest that parents should cease encouraging and praising their bright child, but simply that they should mix in some judicious critical comment when it is appropriate. The failing child *expects* failure and criticism, hence criticism has little effect on him/her her except to confirm his/her worst expectations and reduce his/her effort. But an experience of praise or reward is so striking that s/he works doubly hard to ensure it happens again.

Part III: Bullying and sibling abuse

Teasing and fighting are relatively commonplace problems in and out of the home. However, in some cases, they can take on a worrying sadistic flavour. This behaviour usually starts as a form of verbal aggression which gets on the nerves of the child who is being victimized, leading to a quarrel. This form of bullying is a mental rather than a physical assault.

Sibling violence and abuse

Sibling violence involves an extreme aggressive or violent act directed by one sibling at another and is the most common form of family violence. Frude (1991) states that aside from the pushing, shoving and hair pulling that are very common in children's attacks on one another (see Part II), several cases of extreme aggression, such as babies being thrown down the toilet, assault with knives and scissors, have been reported. The greater the difference in age between the siblings involved in hostile interactions, the more likely it is that the assault and its consequences will approximate abuse of the kind that occurs between adults and children. Indeed, sibling violence is often found in families where there is child physical, sexual and emotional maltreatment by the parents or child sexual abuse by brothers and sisters (see Browne and Herbert, 1996, for a review of the evidence).

Bolton and Bolton (1987) report that families in which serious physical abuse between siblings occurs tend to be chaotic and disorganized; the balance of care and attention is inappropriate. The child perpetrator is frequently an only child who has had to accept the intrusion of new half-siblings. The sibling who perpetrates is often on the 'down side' of the family equation and is seen negatively by the parent(s). The parent tends to be preoccupied with providing attention to the child who is victimized by the sibling. There is a great deal of crisis in the family, centred in particular on the mother. When her time and energy have to be directed elsewhere, the perpetrating child is often asked to serve as 'caregiver' to the child victim and this is just the time when an assault is likely to occur. The discrepancy between the quality of care given to the children is so extreme, obvious, and painful for the perpetrating child, that it is reasonable to hypothesize that abuse toward the seemingly more loved sibling is an effort to get even, a way to express hostility intended for the mother, a device to gain attention, or a strategy to master their own victimization by adopting a perpetrator role.

Age and gender

Research into sibling aggression confirms the belief that, as children grow older, the rates of using aggression or more extreme violence to resolve conflicts between siblings decrease (Steinmetz, 1977; Straus *et al.*, 1988). This could be the result of children becoming better equipped at using verbal skills to settle disputes. Of course, older children do tend to spend more time away from home and this takes them away from potential sibling conflicts.

Steinmetz found that the factors precipitating conflicts varied with age. Younger children were more likely to have conflicts centred on possessions, especially toys. One family reported that, during a one week period, their young children fought over 'the use of a glider, sharing a truck, sharing a tricycle, knocking down one child's building blocks and taking them'. 'Young adolescent conflicts focused on territory, with adolescents becoming very upset if a sibling invaded their personal space. 'They fuss. They say, 'He's sitting on my seat' (Steinmetz, 1977).

At all ages girls are less aggressive than boys, but the differences are relatively small (Gelles and Cornell, 1990). Girls' quarrels tend to be more verbal than physical as compared with boys. Overall, 83 per cent of boys and 74 per cent of girls are physically aggressive toward their brother or sister.

Temperament plays its part on both sides of the coin, being related to the impulsiveness and quick-tempered nature of responses by bullying children (see page 00), as compared with the withdrawal and lack of assertiveness of victims (Herbert, 1991).

Hatred

The role of hatred in sibling aggression is not clear: children may or may not be aggressive towards those whom they hate and aggression may or may not be the outward and visible sign of hatred. Certainly, the intensity of feelings between siblings who are jealous of one another, or the rivalry of step-siblings in reconstituted families, can give every appearance of unmitigated hatred.

Bullying

Bullying, with its intention to *hurt* the victim tends to be a systematically repetitive activity, involving physical and/or psychological (often verbal) harm, instigated by one or more persons against another person who lacks the power, strength or will to resist. Merciless taunting and teasing may be as damaging over the longer term as physical assaults. Children who bully others may be less empathetic to the feelings of others, particularly potential victims; certainly Smith (1990) found that both the typical questionnaire responses, as well as interviews with bullies, revealed that bullies tend to feel positive or neutral about seeing bullying incidents, whereas most other children say they feel bad or unhappy about them.

It is difficult to obtain reliable figures for the prevalence of bullying among children in the home, but they are worryingly high according to surveys carried out on such activities in schools. A study of some 2000 pupils in several middle and secondary schools in South Yorkshire (cited in Smith, 1990) suggests an incidence of up to one in five children being bullied, and up to one in ten children bullying other children. Smith refers to the 'silent nightmare' to describe the fact that half of the victims of bullying kept their suffering to themselves. Children who are aggressive at school tend to be aggressive at home; after non-compliance (the flouting of authority), aggression is one of the most common complaints of adults who have to rear, care for, or teach difficult children.

Cognitive and social skill deficits

Social competence in children is commonly defined as a five-stage processing model:

1. encoding the stimulus situation;
2. interpreting it;
3. searching for suitable responses;
4. evaluating the best response;
5. enacting the chosen response.

Any 'deficit' in social competence would be ascribed to failure in one or more of these stages. Research in the US suggests that highly aggressive children tend to encode situations as hostile (that is, more readily attributing hostile intentions to others), and to generate fewer non-hostile responses (see Hollin and Trower, 1986). It has been argued that in children who bully others, it is not so much that they lack social skills in the information-processing sense, but that they simply have different values and goals which give direction (or a lack of direction, some would say) to their social encounters.

Adaptive/maladaptive functioning

Bullying behaviour could be considered as behaviour which might have been appropriate for the individual performing it at one time, or in certain circumstances, but which is *no longer* socially acceptable, or appropriate *in any circumstances* because of the harm it does to others. An example of the latter comes from interviews with bullies which often suggest that bullies view the playground as a tough place where you need to dominate or humiliate others in order not to be so treated yourself (Smith, 1990).

Part IV: A therapeutic approach to aggression

As a general principle, it is clear that the maintenance of aggressive behaviour is in large part dependent on its consequences. Aggressive actions that have 'rewarding' consequences (and this might include a frustrated parent letting off steam) tend to be repeated, whereas those that are unrewarded or punished are likely to be reduced in frequency, or eliminated. In the case of habitually coercive families, the cues or messages are frequently negative ones, such as incessant criticism, nagging, crying, shouting and so on.

Punishment: a critique

The position taken by Patterson (1982), and he qualifies it carefully, is that the control of antisocial behaviour requires the contingent use of some kind of punishment. This claim seems on the surface, at least, to run counter to the many studies from developmental psychology that investigated parental reports about their punitive practices. They consistently show a positive correlation with antisocial child behaviour (Feshbach, 1964). Parents of problem children report that they use punishment *more frequently* than parents of normal children; their punitive practices are also more likely to be extreme. As we have seen in this section, the parents of socially aggressive children do punish more often in reaction to sibling and problem child aggressive behaviour.

The modelling-frustration hypothesis

This was formulated by Bandura (1973). He maintains that in exercising punitive control, prohibitive agents model aggressive styles of behaviour not unlike those they wish to discourage in others. Recipients may, on later occasions, adopt similar aggressive solutions in coping with the problems confronting them. He adds that although the direction of causal relationships cannot be unequivocally established from correlational data, it is clear from controlled studies that aggressive modelling breeds aggression. Here then is the seed corn for intergenerational violence, but why does aggressive behaviour that is punished not diminish or disappear as would be predicted from learning theory?

Berkowitz (1993) emphasizes the likelihood that it is *the kind of punishment* used by parents of aggressive children that may be ineffective. He makes a case for the necessity of punishing aggressive child behaviours, but in the context of being a warm, loving parent, who uses reasoning or explanations in conjunction with *nonviolent* punishment, such as time-out. Patterson (*op. cit.*) finds himself in agreement with Berkowitz's position, one which reflects the Patterson team's conclusion from a decade of intervention studies with families of aggressive children. Time-out and analogous consequences (such as extra work or loss of privileges) are definitely aversive; however they are *not* violent and Patterson vouches for their relative effectiveness. Certainly, there is overwhelming evidence that extremes of physical punishment perpetrated against a background of uncaring indifference or outright rejection, constitutes the slippery slope for the creation of a violent youngster.

Contracts

We have seen that in coercive families the cues or messages are frequently negative ones. Communication between members may not be so much aversive as impoverished or practically non-existent. Where family systems include behaviour control by the use of verbal and/or physical pain, they are likely to produce children who exhibit frequent (high rate) aggressive actions. Coercive interactions, maintained by negative reinforcement, are most likely to operate in closed social systems where the child must learn to cope with aversive stimuli such as incessant criticism.

This is where contracts come in. And certainly one way of increasing positively reinforcing communications while reducing punitive interactions is by the practitioner sitting down to work out a contract for members of the family. The discussion, negotiation and compromise in such therapist-led situations introduces the family to an important means of resolving interpersonal conflicts and tensions and to enhanced communication, which they may have experienced only rarely.

The following guidelines might be followed in planning the contract:

➤   Keep the discussion positive. Recriminations are unavoidable, but the volume should be kept down and negative complaints turned into positive suggestions.
➤   Be very specific in spelling out desired actions.
➤   Pay attention to the details of privileges and conditions for both parties. They should (a) be important, not trivial; and (b) make sense to the person(s) involved.

Strategies

Some suggested strategies to discuss with parents with regard to behaviour management are provided in the Hints for Parents handout at the end of this guide.

References

Bandura, A. (1973). *Aggression: A Social Learning Analysis.* Englewood Cliffs, NJ: Prentice-Hall.

Baumrind, D. (1971). Current patterns of parental authority. *Developmental Psychology Monographs, 4, (1)* Part 2, 1–103.

Berkowitz, L. (1993). *Aggression: Its Causes, Consequences and Control.* New York: McGraw-Hill.

Bolton, F.G. and Bolton, S.R. (1987). *Working with Violent Families: A guide for clinical and legal practitioners.* New York: Sage.

Browne, K. and Herbert, M. (1996). *Preventing Family Violence.* Chichester: Wiley.

Dunn, J. and Kendrick, C. (1982). *Siblings: Love, envy and understanding.* Cambridge, MA: Harvard University Press.

Feshbach, S. (1964). The function of aggression and the regulation of the aggressive drive. *Psychological Review, 71,* 257–272.

Frude, N. (1991). *Understanding Family Problems: A Psychological Approach.* Chichester: Wiley.

Gelles, R.J. and Cornell, C.P. (1990). *Intimate Violence in Families,* 2nd edn. Beverley Hills, CA: Sage.

Herbert, M. (1987a). *Conduct Disorders of Childhood and Adolescence,* 2nd edn. Chichester: John Wiley.

Herbert, M. (1987b) *Behavioural Treatment of Children with Problems: A practice manual.* London: Academic Press.

Herbert, M. (1989). *Discipline: A positive guide for parents.* Oxford: Basil Blackwell.

Herbert, M. (1991). *Clinical Child Psychology: Social learning, development and behaviour.* Chichester: John Wiley.

Herbert, M. (1993). *Working with Children and The Children Act.* Leicester: BPS Books (The British Psychological Society).

Hollin, C.R. and Trower, P. (1986). *Handbook of Social Skills Training.* (2 vols). Oxford: Pergamon Press.

Olweus, D. (1989). Prevalence and incidence in the study of antisocial behaviour: Definitions and measurements. In M.W. Klein (Ed.) *Cross National Research in Self-Reported Crime and Delinquency.* Dordrecht: Kluwes.

Patterson, G. (1982). *Coercive Family Process.* Eugene, OR: Castalia.

Smith, P.K. (1990) The Silent Nightmare: Bullying and victimization in school peer groups. Paper read to The British Psychological Society London Conference.

Steinmetz, S.K. (1977). Family violence: Past, present and future. In M.B. Sussman and S.K. Steinmetz (Eds) *Handbook of Marriage and the Family.* New York: Plenum.

Straus, M., Gelles, R.J. and Steinmetz, S.K. (1988). *Behind Closed Doors: Violence in the American Family.* Beverley Hills, CA: Sage.

Webster Stratton, C. and Herbert, M. (1994). *Troubled Families: Problem Children.* Chichester: Wiley.

West, D.J. and Farrington, D.P. (1973). *Who Becomes Delinquent?* London: Heinemann Educational.

Further reading

Davis, L.V. and Carlson, B.E. (1987). Observation of spouse abuse: what happens to the children? *Journal of Interpersonal Violence, 2,* 278–291.

Dunn, J. (1984). *Sisters and Brothers.* London: Fontana.

Steinmetz, S. (1978). Battered parents. *Society, 15*(5), 54–55.

Appendix I: Frequency Chart

Child's name:
Date:
Week no.:

Target behaviours:

1. _____
2. _____
3. _____

	Monday	Tuesday	Wednes-day	Thurs-day	Friday	Saturday	Sunday
6–8 a.m.							
8–10 a.m.							
10–12 a.m.							
12–2 p.m.							
2–4 p.m.							
4–6 p.m.							
6–8 p.m.							
8–10 p.m.							
10–12 p.m.							
12–2 a.m.							
2–4 a.m.							
4–6 a.m.							

Appendix II: ABC Record

Child's name:
Child's age:
Date:

Behaviour being recorded:

Date and time	Antecedent: what happened beforehand?	Behaviour: what did your child do?	Consequences: what was the end result? (i) What did you do (e.g. ignore, argue, scold, smack, etc.)? (ii) How did s/he react?	Describe your feelings

Hints for Parents

Give your child a chance to cool down

From what we know from research into the problem of aggression, it seems that scoldings administered in the heat of anger are likely to perpetuate the spiral of frustration → resentment → anger → aggression → counter-aggression. It is no use trying to reason with a child when s/he is in the middle of a tantrum. Turn away from the persistent tantrum or walk out on it. When your child is calm again, s/he should be told *why* the behaviour was unacceptable.

Restrain him/her firmly and as gently as possible

You cannot always afford to ignore a child's aggression. Put your arms around him/her firmly so that s/he cannot lash out. (This is called *passive inhibition.*)

Reduce aversive stimuli

It is crucial to attempt to change the circumstances which trigger off your child's aggressive behaviour. It often stems from frustrating, depriving or provocative experiences caused by other people or life circumstances. Admittedly, this is easier said than done.

Reduce triggers or signals which set the stage for aggressive behaviour

The absence of a supervising adult may be the signal for a child to threaten or hit another in order to take away (say) their possessions, or just for the pleasure of bullying. Better organized supervision in the playground or home would be one response to this situation.

Reduce exposure to aggressive models

If your child is mixing with someone whom you know is a bully and who is providing an example of aggressive behaviour, it is advisable to detach your child from this relationship as soon as possible. Also, could *you* be displaying hostile attitudes and aggressive actions?

Provide models of non-aggressive behaviour

You could encourage acceptable alternatives to aggression by exposing your child to children who display peaceable actions; this can be effective especially when s/he sees that they obtain rewards for such behaviour. To teach a child new patterns of behaviour, give him/her the opportunity to observe a person performing the desired actions. This is called modelling, and can be used effectively in the following situations:

> ➤ to acquire new or alternative patterns of behaviour from the model, such as social skills, self-control, which your child has never shown;
> ➤ to increase or decrease responses already in the child's repertoire through the demonstration of appropriate behaviour.

Skills training

Many children lack some of the skills required to function in society in a satisfactory manner. Consequently, they may behave aggressively in response to a variety of frustrations and humiliations. If such children can be helped to become more competent, then they may resort to aggression less. For example, you might teach your child the skill of being more assertive; that is, to protect his/her own rights in a capable and confident manner, without denying the rights of others by being aggressive or neglectful towards them.

Provide rewards for non-aggressive behaviour while penalizing aggressive actions

Some parents make undesirable behaviour unworthwhile, as in the following example.

Antecedents	Behaviour	Consequences
Johnnie wanted to go to the park. Dad said there wasn't time before tea.	Johnnie kicked and shouted, lay on the floor and screamed.	Dad ignored his tantrum; eventually Johnnie calmed down and began to play.

By reacting to the tantrum, Johnnie's father would have made the undesirable behaviour (e.g. aggression) worthwhile and thus more likely to recur!

Just as behaviour that is reinforced (rewarded) tends to recur, so behaviour that is not reinforced or is punished tends to be discontinued. By 'rewards' we do not mean expensive, tangible things, nor by 'punishments' do we mean things that are physical, harsh or painful. We are trying to help children to see that certain behaviours produce desirable consequences (such as praise, approval, esteem, treats, privileges), while other forms of behaviour do not.

What we have is a rough and ready rule of thumb:

Acceptable behaviour + reinforcement (reward) = more acceptable behaviour

Acceptable behaviour + no reinforcement = less acceptable behaviour

Unacceptable behaviour + reinforcement (a reward) = more unacceptable behaviour

Unacceptable behaviour + no reinforcement = less unacceptable behaviour

A prerequisite for training children is the necessity for you as parents to provide meaningful, positive attention to your child in a manner that is consistent, while ignoring inappropriate actions. It goes without saying that if children love, trust and respect their parents – in other words, *identify* with them – their desire to please them (by and large) makes parents' rewards and sanctions very powerful.

A non-aggressive punishment provides conditions which signal to the child that his/her aggressive behaviour is *not* about to produce a pay-off. Indeed, it is likely to lead to negative outcomes (penalties). The provision of such messages (in technical jargon called *discriminative stimuli*) as part of your tactics may bring aggression under control while you encourage more acceptable alternative behaviour.

Time-out

Children sometimes need time to bring their self-control into play. A period in which they can think about their aggressive behaviour and how self-defeating it is, may do the trick. Explain to them how it leads to unhappiness for her/himself, not to mention others. For example, it may be necessary to remove your child from a group (by letting him/her watch an activity but not participate) if s/he persists in disrupting the fun. Other methods can be devised to make bad-tempered behaviour costly. Nothing stops a scene as effectively as removing a child from an audience. This age-old and very effective method has been blessed with a technical term – 'time-out from positive reinforcement'.

Time-out has been shown to be an effective disciplinary method. It is intended to reduce the frequency of behaviour such as aggression by making sure that the child has very little opportunity to acquire any reinforcement, or rewards. In practice we can choose from three forms of time-out:

1. *Activity time-out*: where the child is simply barred from joining in an enjoyable activity but still allowed to observe it – for example, having misbehaved s/he is made to sit out of a game.
2. *Room time-out*: where s/he is removed from an enjoyable activity, not allowed to observe it, but not totally isolated – for example, having misbehaved, sitting in a 'time-out' chair at the far end of the sitting room or a classroom.
3. *Seclusion time-out*: where s/he is socially isolated in a situation away from the rewards of the situation.

Time-out may last from three to five minutes. In practice, 'activity' or 'room' time-out should always be preferred before any form of 'seclusion' time-out. Warn your child *in advance* about those of his/her behaviours which are considered inappropriate and the consequences that will follow them. It is helpful to discuss with a professional *in advance* the range of issues that may arise from the use of time-out. For example, time-out is quite likely to lead to tantrums or rebellious behaviour such as crying, screaming, and physical assaults. With older children, who can physically resist you, the method may simply not be feasible. When the behaviour to be eliminated is an extraordinarily compelling one that *demands* attention (reinforcement) from those present, or when time-out is difficult to administer because the child is strong and protesting, an equivalent may be instituted by removing the sources of reinforcement/reward from him/her. So if you are a major source of reinforcement, you should remove yourself, together with a magazine, to the bathroom when the child's temper tantrums erupt, coming out only when all is quiet.

Response–cost

Response–cost procedures involve a penalty being awarded for failure to complete a desired response. This may involve forfeiting rewards currently available – failure to do homework results in the loss of television privileges. It is a feature of the **collaborative approach** that with this, as with other methods, parents help the practitioner problem-solve – that is, to come up with appropriate costs and rewards. This was used in the case of Matthew, a hyperactive boy, who was extremely disruptive and noisy. He made life miserable for his older brothers and sisters while they read or watched television by constantly interrupting them, making loud humming and wailing noises and banging things. The response–cost method was explained to his parents in the following way: 'To stop your child from acting in an unacceptable way, you need to arrange for him to bring to an end a significantly unpleasant consequence, by changing the behaviour in the desired direction'. The parents worked out the following scenario for Matthew.

A bottle of marbles representing Matthew's weekly pocket money, plus a bonus, was placed on the mantelpiece. Each instance of misbehaviour cost a marble (the equivalent of a specific sum of money). In a good week, Matthew could increase his pocket money quite substantially; in a bad week it could be reduced to zero. Of course, the 'cost' of misbehaviour was highly visible to him. As always, sanctions were to be balanced by rewards, since punishment alone tells children what *not* to do, not what they *are* expected to do. An extension of the range of rewards for therapeutic interventions is enshrined in the so-called Premack principle (better known as 'Granny's Rule'), where a preferred behaviour is made to connect with correctly performing a non-preferred behaviour. This principle, when applied by his parents, required Matthew to play quietly for set periods, timed with a kitchen timer, and if he did this successfully, he was rewarded by stickers. These could be exchanged for time on a computer game.

Logical consequences

If you ensure (within limits of safety) that your child is allowed to experience the consequences of his/her own actions, this becomes an effective means of modifying behaviour. If your child is destructive with a possession and, for example, it breaks, s/he is more likely to learn to be careful if s/he has to do without it. If you always replace the toy s/he is likely to continue to be destructive.

Unfortunately, from the point of view of the parents' self-interest, children are frequently not left to experience the consequences of their own misbehaviour. Against their own and the child's best interests parents intervene to protect their offspring from reality. The result, however, of this kindness is that the implications (outcomes) of the situation often do not become apparent to the child and they go on committing the same misdeeds over and over again. A good deal of discussion and debate is required here. To what extent (particularly with toddlers and teenagers) should you intervene (interfere?) to protect your child from the inevitable risks of life? To what extent is your child allowed to learn from experience – the hard way?

Self-management training

There are techniques which can help to strengthen self-control. Training involves making your child aware of the circumstances in which s/he gets angry, and then moves through a series of stages. First, you would model the performance of a task, making appropriate and positive self-statements, such as 'Think first, act afterwards'; 'It's not worth losing my temper'; 'I'll count to ten and stay calm'. Your child then practises the same behaviour, gradually moving to whispered, and eventually silent, self-instruction. Children are encouraged to use these self-statements so that they can observe, evaluate and reinforce appropriate behaviour in themselves.

Something worth remembering

Children whose parents set firm limits for them grow up with more self-esteem and confidence than those who are allowed to get away with behaving in any way they like, notably with aggression. It is important, however, to give youngsters some freedom of choice within reasonable limits. Not surprisingly, children are likely to complain and compare themselves with other children when the limits are set down and insisted on. However, there is clear evidence to show that children realize their parents are firm *because they care.* They know, deep down, that they cannot cope alone. They need to know someone has charge of their lives so that they can learn about and experiment with life from a safe base. Children who get their own way all the time often interpret such permissiveness as indifference; they feel nothing they do is important enough for their parents to bother about.